NEPAL

By Theia Lake and
Joanne Mattern

Published in 2025 by Cavendish Square Publishing, LLC
2544 Clinton Street, Buffalo, NY 14224

Second Edition

Website: cavendishsq.com

Cataloging-in-Publication Data

Names: Lake, Theia. | Mattern, Joanne, 1963-.
Title: Nepal / Theia Lake and Joanne Mattern.
Description: Second edition. | Buffalo, NY : Cavendish Square Publishing, 2025. | Series: Exploring world cultures | Includes glossary and index.
Identifiers: ISBN 9781502670885 (pbk.) | ISBN 9781502670892 (library bound) | ISBN 9781502670908 (ebook)
Subjects: LCSH: Nepal--Juvenile literature.
Classification: LCC DS493.4 L35 2025 | DDC 954.96--dc23

Writers: Joanne Mattern; Theia Lake (second edition)
Editor: Theresa Emminizer
Copyeditor: Danielle Haynes
Designer: Andrea Davison-Bartolotta

The photographs in this book are used by permission and through the courtesy of: Cover hadynyah/iStockphoto.com; p. 4 toiletroom/Shutterstock.com; p. 5 Pisit Rapitpunt/Shutterstock.com; p. 6 Peter Hermes Furian/Shutterstock.com; p. 7 Daniel Prudek/Shutterstock.com; p. 8 Jasper Neupane/Shutterstock.com; p. 9 dinesh magar/Shutterstock.com; pp. 10, 12 gorkhe1980/Shutterstock.com; p. 11 Aryan Dhimal/ZUMA Press Wire/Alamy Stock Photo; p. 13 Boyloso/Shutterstock.com; p. 15 (top) Wang LiQiang/Shutterstock.com; pp. 15 (bottom), 18 PACO COMO/Shutterstock.com; p. 16 Keshav Dulal/Shutterstock.com; p. 17 Travel Stock/Shutterstock.com; p. 19 Nabaraj Regmi/Shutterstock.com; p. 20 Richie Chan/Shutterstock.com; p. 21 TanyaBond/Shutterstock.com; p. 22 d_odin/Shutterstock.com; p. 23 Lisa Strachan/Shutterstock.com; p. 24 Marion Carniel/Shutterstock.com; p. 25 Samyak Shrestha/Shutterstock.com; p. 26 Fotos593/Shutterstock.com; p. 27 Iryna Hromotska/Shutterstock.com; p. 28 Nickolas warner/Shutterstock.com; p. 29 Alivenishant/Shutterstock.com.

CPSIA compliance information: Batch #CS25CSQ: For further information contact Cavendish Square Publishing LLC at 1-877-980-4450.

Printed in the United States of America

CONTENTS

Introduction 4
Chapter 1 Geography 6
Chapter 2 History 8
Chapter 3 Government 10
Chapter 4 The Economy 12
Chapter 5 The Environment 14
Chapter 6 The People Today 16
Chapter 7 Lifestyle 18
Chapter 8 Religion 20
Chapter 9 Language 22
Chapter 10 Arts and Festivals 24
Chapter 11 Fun and Play 26
Chapter 12 Food 28
Glossary 30
Find Out More 31
Index 32

INTRODUCTION

Nepal is a beautiful, mountainous country in Asia. It has a long, rich history that's been shaped by its unique, or one-of-a-kind, geography.

People who make their home in Nepal are called Nepalese people. Nepalese people come from many different **cultural** backgrounds. They speak many different languages and have special **traditions** and celebrations.

Boudhanath Stupa is a Buddhist monument in Kathmandu, the capital of Nepal.

The Hindu and Buddhist religions, or belief sysems, play a big part in life in Nepal. Nepalese art, music, and architecture, or buildings, show the importance of these beliefs. You can find beautiful temples, or religious buildings, in Nepal.

Nepal is also home to wildlife such as snow leopards, Bengal tigers, and Asian elephants. Many visitors are drawn to Nepal because of the Himalayan mountain range.

Nepal's long history, tasty food, amazing sights, and multicultural **heritage** make it a special place for those who live there and those who visit.

Each year, thousands of people travel to Nepal to climb Mount Annapurna, pictured here.

GEOGRAPHY

Nepal is a landlocked country, meaning it's surrounded by land. Nepal is bordered by India in the west, south, and east. Tibet, which is part of China, lies to the north.

The Himalayas stretch across Nepal's northern border. Many of the world's tallest mountains are in Nepal, including Mount Everest. The Karnali, Kosi, and Gandak Rivers flow down from the Himalayas.

This map of Nepal shows its capital and its borders.

The southern part of Nepal is a flat area called the Tarai (or Terai). The climate, or weather, here is hot and wet. The Tarai is covered with **marshes** and forests.

THE HIMALAYAS

Around 75 percent of Nepal is covered in mountains! The mountains in the Great Himalayas (part of the larger Himalayan range) vary in height from 14,000 feet (4,267 m) to more than 29,000 feet (8,839 m) above sea level. For the most part, this area is uninhabited, meaning no one lives there.

HISTORY

A group called the Kirat came to Nepal during the 8th century BCE. Later, several different groups ruled Nepal. One of the most important were the Mallas. They ruled from the 10th to the 18th centuries CE.

*The Sky Caves, shown here, are **ancient**, man-made caves in Mustang, Nepal.*

THE SKY CAVES

Nepal's Sky Caves are believed to be over 2,000 years old! They were made by the Lopa tribe and had many different uses over the years. The ancient artwork within the caves can still be seen today.

In time, the area around Kathmandu was divided into three kingdoms. A nearby king named Prithvi Narayan Shah spent more than 20 years **conquering** these kingdoms. By 1768, he had combined these kingdoms into the nation of Nepal.

In 1816, the British conquered Nepal. Nepal won its independence in 1923. Between 1950 and 2007, Nepal was ruled by kings. Nepal became a **republic** in 2008.

FACT!

There are many legends, or cultural stories that have been passed down, about Nepal's long history.

Bhaktapur Durbar Square, pictured here, is home to many important historical monuments.

GOVERNMENT

After winning independence from Britain, Nepal was ruled by kings for many years. That changed in 2008 when a new government was formed.

In 2015, Nepal made a new **constitution**. Modern Nepal is governed based on that constitution. A president is the head of state. There's also a Council of Ministers, which is a group of political leaders led by a prime minister. The prime minister is the head of government.

Nepal's flag, shown here, is the only national flag in the world that's not four-sided!

The country is grouped into seven provinces, which are like states. The legislature makes the country's laws.

MAOIST INSURGENCY

The Maoists were a political party—a group with ideas about government—in Nepal. In 1996, the Maoists led an insurgency, or a bloody effort to overthrow the monarchy. The insurgency went on until 2006. During that time, nearly 12,000 Nepalese people were killed.

FACT!

Every Nepalese citizen who is at least 18 years old can vote in all elections.

Ram Chandra Poudel, pictured here, became Nepal's third president in March 2023.

THE ECONOMY

Nepal is one of the least developed countries in the world. That means it doesn't have a high level of **industrialization** or large **economy**.

Nepal has few natural resources, or things found in nature that humans can use, and limited land that can be used for growing crops. The main crops are rice, corn, wheat, and potatoes, but farmers can't produce enough food to feed Nepal's people. Instead, the government must get food from other countries.

These farm workers are harvesting, or gathering, a crop of tea leaves.

There are few industries in Nepal. The most common are carpet-making and handmade cloth, wood, and leather crafts. Tourism also contributes, or adds, to Nepal's economy.

TOURISM

Many people travel to Nepal to see its wonderful sights and natural beauty. Tourists, or visitors, are drawn to Nepal because of the mountain climbing, hiking, and bird watching it offers. Many people in Nepal work as tour guides. They also work in restaurants and hotels that serve tourists.

FACT!

Nepal imports, or brings in, goods from many other countries. They include fuel and building materials.

Nepalese currency, or money, is called rupees.

THE ENVIRONMENT

Nepal is well known for its stunning land and natural beauty. The country has lots of thick forests of bamboo, pine trees, and oak trees. Many different flowers grow in the hot, wet climate, or weather.

Tigers, leopards, elephants, rhinoceroses, and deer live in the Tarai of Nepal. Crocodiles and dolphins swim in the rivers, while storks and cranes live in the marshes. The hills and mountains are also full of life. Himalayan black bears live in the mountains, and so do mountain goats and red pandas. The mountains are also home to **endangered** snow leopards.

NATIONAL PARKS

Many endangered animals and native plants are protected in Nepal's national parks. Chitwan National Park, founded in 1973, was the first national park in Nepal. It's part of the Tarai. It's home to some of last wild single-horned Asiatic rhinoceroses and Bengal tigers on Earth.

The Himalayan monal is the national bird of Nepal. It has beautiful, brightly colored feathers.

FACT!

A hot wind called the Loo sometimes blows across the Tarai. The Loo can raise temperatures as high as 113 degrees Fahrenheit (45 degrees Celsius).

This family of Asian elephants lives in Bardiya National Park in Nepal.

THE PEOPLE TODAY

There are many different **ethnic** groups in Nepal. Some come from Indian and Tibetan backgrounds. The Newar are the Indigenous, or Native, people of the Kathmandu Valley in Nepal. Hill people, who live in the lower mountains in central and western Nepal, include ethnic groups called the Gurung, Tamang, Rai, and Limbu.

FACT!
About 30 million people live in Nepal today.

A Gurung woman is weaving cotton on a sunny day in the Annapurna mountains.

The Sherpas are the most famous of the hill people. Sherpas live in the high mountains of the Himalayas. They often serve as guides and helpers for people trying to climb Mount Everest, Earth's highest mountain.

THE CASTE SYSTEM

Historically, Nepal's people were divided into four groups called castes: Brahmin, Kshatriya, Vaishya, and Shudra. The higher the caste, the more comfortable life a person tended to have. The caste system was officially abolished, or ended, but it continues to be part of people's lives.

A Sherpa boy is sitting with his cow in Puiyan, in the Everest region.

LIFESTYLE

Life in Nepal differs based on one's ethnic group. For most, however, family is very important. Most people in Nepal live in large family groups, which include children, parents, grandparents, aunts, uncles, and cousins.

FACT!
Music, dance, art, and religion are important parts of the cultural life of Nepalese people.

Many traditional Nepalese homes (like the one pictured here) are made of mud or stone.

Many marriages in Nepal are arranged. That means that family members bring the bride and groom together. Some couples don't meet until the wedding! Although marriages for love do take place in Nepal, arranged marriage is still a big part of Nepalese culture. Weddings usually last for several days and include lots of colorful clothes.

COUNTRY LIFE, CITY LIFE

Many families live in the country. They grow their own food and trade with other people for goods. People in the cities live in small houses or apartments. They buy food and other goods in stores. People use bicycles, buses, and taxies to get around.

This woman is dancing at a wedding in the countryside of Nepal.

RELIGION

Most Nepalese people are Hindu. Hindu practices are part of everyday life. Hindus believe in hundreds of different gods. Reincarnation, or living many lives, is an important part of Hindu belief.

FACT!

About 81 percent of the people in Nepal are Hindu. Eight percent are Buddhist, and 5 percent are Muslim.

Pashupatinath Temple, pictured here, is a religious site in Nepal.

Buddhism is also popular in Nepal. Buddhism is based on the teachings of Siddhartha Gautama, who was called the Buddha. He left a life of comfort to find the meaning of life. Buddhists believe that life is an cycle of birth, death, and rebirth.

Hinduism and Buddhism are blended into Nepalese culture.

PRAYER FLAGS

When you see pictures of Nepal, you often see colorful flags waving in the wind. These are prayer flags. Each flag has a mantra, or prayer, written on it. Buddhists believe prayer flags bring happiness and peace to those who see them.

This Buddhist monk is praying on a mountain in the Himalayas.

LANGUAGE

There are 123 languages spoken in Nepal! The official language of Nepal is called Nepali. Nepali is a lot like the Hindi language that is spoken in India. Nepali script, or written language, shares a lot in common with other Indian languages. Nepali first appeared in the 12th century. This language is taught in schools, along with English.

This Buddha statue has Nepali writing beneath it.

Most people in Nepal also speak a local language, or dialect. Maithili, Limbu, and Nepal Bhasa are some of the other Nepalese languages.

FACT!

The Nepali language is spoken by more than 17 million people.

Buddhist prayer wheels, like those pictured here, have words carved on them.

NAMASTE

"Namaste" is an important word in Nepal. It comes from the Sanskrit language and is a respectful greeting or thank you. Namaste means "the divine (godlike) in me greets the divine in you." This is usually said while holding one's palms together and bowing one's head.

ARTS AND FESTIVALS

Nepal is home to many beautiful paintings and sculptures. There are many beautiful statues all over Nepal, especially in Kathmandu. Most of Nepal's art is based on religion. Paintings and statues show religious ideas and important figures.

FACT!

Buddha Jayanti celebrates the birth and life of the Buddha, who was born in what's now Nepal.

This artist is painting a **mandala** in Kathmandu.

Dashain is the biggest holiday in Nepal. It celebrates good winning over evil. Dashain celebrations last for 15 days.

Tihar is a fall festival that comes right after Dashain. During Tihar, people light their homes to honor Lakshmi, the goddess of wealth and good fortune.

MUSIC

Music is very popular in Nepal. People play flutes, drums, and a traditional horn called a *shehnai*. Western music and instruments, such as guitars and banjos, are also popular. Music is a big part of any festival, wedding, or other celebration.

The Maitidevi Temple in Kathmandu is decorated for the Tihar festival.

FUN AND PLAY

Football, or soccer, is the most popular sport in Nepal. Cricket is also very popular. Cricket is played with a bat and a ball and involves sets of sticks called wickets. People in Nepal also enjoy *kabaddi*, which is a type of tag played by two teams.

FACT!

Nepal's landscape offers many different outdoor sporting activities including hiking, mountain climbing, and rafting.

These young Nepalese Buddhists are playing soccer.

Board games are popular too. Nepal's most famous board game is called *bagh-chal*, or "tigers and goats." The player who is the tiger uses their pieces to jump over the other player's goats. The goats try to trap the tigers.

FLYING KITES

Kite flying is enjoyed by children and adults. People have kite battles, where they try to snap the string of another kite with the sharp string of their own kite. During the festival of Dashain, kites carry messages of joy and hope into the sky.

This is what a traditional bagh-chal set looks like.

FOOD

Nepalese food shows off the country's multicultural heritage. *Dal bhat* is the most popular dish. It's a spicy lentil soup with rice and vegetables. Potatoes and squash are also common foods. Many people enjoy potatoes dipped in salt and hot chilies.

Momos are another tasty food. These are small envelopes of white **dough** stuffed with vegetables, lamb, or chicken.

This is a picture of dal baht. It's thought of as the national dish of Nepal.

Yomari is a sweet dish made with rice dough and a paste of coconut, sesame seeds, and molasses.

FACT!
Rice is a major food in Nepal. It's eaten at every meal.

The most common meats in Nepal come from buffalo, goats, or yaks. It's against the Hindu religion to eat beef.

NEWARI CUISINE

Juju dhau, chatamari, and choila are a few of the many tasty Newari dishes. Juju dhau is a thick, creamy yogurt made with buffalo milk. Chatamari is made with meat, eggs, onions, and spices. Choila is a spicy dish made with water buffalo meat.

GLOSSARY

ancient: Very old or belonging to much earlier times.

conquer: To take over a place or group of people.

constitution: The basic laws by which a country, state, or group is governed.

cultural: Having to do with the beliefs and ways of life of a certain group of people.

dough: A mix of flour and water.

economy: The way in which goods and services are made, sold, and used in a country or area.

endangered: At risk of going extinct, or dying out completely.

ethnic: Of or relating to large groups of people who have the same cultural background and ways of life.

heritage: The traditions and beliefs that are part of the history of a group or nation.

industrialization: The process of a country becoming more industrial, or using machines to do work that was once done by people.

mandala: A symbolic design representing the universe in Hindu and Buddhist traditions.

marsh: An area of soft, wet land.

republic: A country governed by elected representatives and an elected leader.

tradition: A way of thinking, behaving, or doing something that's been used by people in a particular society for a long time.

FIND OUT MORE

Books

Douglas, Ed. *Himalaya: A Human History*. New York, NY: W. W. Norton & Company, Inc., 2021.

Haynes, Danielle. *Scaling Mount Everest*. Buffalo, NY: PowerKids Press, 2024.

Mayhew, Bradley, Joe Bindloss, Lindsay Brown, Stuart Butler, Tsering Lama. *Lonely Planet Nepal*. Oakland, CA: Lonely Planet Publishing, 2023.

Websites

Britannica: Nepal
www.britannica.com/place/Nepal
Learn more about Nepal's history.

Nepal Tourism Board
ntb.gov.np
Check out all there is to see and do in Nepal.

Video

"7 UNESCO World Heritage Sites of Kathmandu Valley"
www.youtube.com/watch?v=lnTp349Mx9k
See some of the most famous sites in this part of Nepal.

INDEX

A
agriculture, 12
arts, 5, 8, 18, 24, 25

B
Bardiya National Park, 15
Bhaktapur Durbar Square, 9
Boudhanath Stupa, 4

C
caste, 17
Chitwan National Park, 14
climate/weather, 15
cuisine/food, 5, 28, 29

E
economy, 12, 13
ethnicity, 16, 17, 18

G
government, 9, 10, 11, 12

H
Himalayas, 5, 6, 7, 17

K
Kathmandu, 4, 9, 24

L
language, 4, 22, 23

M
Maitidevi Temple, 25
Mount Annapurna, 5
Mount Everest, 6, 7, 17

P
Pashupatinath Temple, 20
plants, 7, 14
Poudel, Ram Chandra, 11

R
religion, 4, 5, 20, 21, 22, 23, 24, 25, 29

S
Shah, Prithvi Narayan, 9
sports, 26

T
Tarai, 7, 14
tourism, 5, 13

W
wildlife, 5, 13, 14, 15